Drive Toward the Future

Anne Kaske

Contents

Rigby

A Harcourt Achieve Imprint

www.Rigby.com

1-800-531-5015

Introduction

Can you imagine life without cars? How would you get to school every day? How would you go to other places, such as stores or parks? How would you visit friends and relatives in other cities or states? Three hundred years ago, you probably would have walked to school, and traveling to another city would have been a big adventure!

The automobile has made it easy to go to school or visit your relatives in another city. But it wasn't always that way. Before automobiles existed, people had to walk or ride in carriages pulled by horses, and it took a very long time to travel from place to place. However, once the first automobile was built, cars quickly changed how people lived. Today you and the people around you can take advantage of the technology that made the automobile possible.

Chapter 1

Start Your Steam Engines!

The first vehicle appeared in the 1700s and had a steam engine. In 1769 a French engineer, Nicolas-Joseph Cugnot, attached a steam engine to a three-wheeled tractor. The engine had a boiler, which is a metal container where water is heated by a furnace. Steam was produced, and the steam created pressure that turned parts of the engine. The moving parts of the engine turned the wheels of the tractor.

Cugnot's steam tractor

About ten years later, a man from England, Richard Trevithick, built a four-wheeled steam car that was designed to carry passengers.

The first steam cars were noisy and smoky, and the pressure from the steam sometimes caused the engines to explode! The cars also damaged the roads and were expensive to repair, so many people still preferred to travel by horse and carriage or train.

 Trevithick's steam car

The Red Flag Law

England's inventors stopped working on steam engines after a law was passed in 1865 stating that steam cars could only travel 6 kilometers (4 miles) per hour in the country and 3 kilometers (2 miles) per hour in the city. The driver of a steam car also had to warn people that the car was coming. Someone had to walk ahead of the car, carrying a red flag during the day and a red lantern at night.

Speeding Up

Even the first race cars seem slow compared to today's regular cars. In 1895 the first automobile race took place in France. Cars raced 732 miles round-trip from Paris to Bordeaux, and the winners drove at an average speed of only 15 miles per hour.

Today, race car driving is a popular sport. The average speed of cars that race in some of the biggest races—the Grand Prix, the Indianapolis 500, and NASCAR races—is over 200 miles per hour.

Chapter 2

A New Kind of Engine

It wasn't until 1885 that a new kind of engine would replace the steam engine and change the future of transportation. Two German men, Gottlieb Daimler and Karl Benz, were separately working on engines that did not use steam. Both men developed engines that burned gasoline. Because the gasoline and air burned inside the engine, this kind of engine is now called an internal-combustion engine.

Karl Benz

Gottlieb Daimler

Internal-combustion engine

8

How an Internal-Combustion Engine Works

Most internal-combustion engines work in four steps, or strokes.

Step 1: Intake Stroke

The intake valve works like a door—when the intake valve is open, gasoline flows in, and a round object, called a piston, moves down into a tube, called a cylinder. This downward movement sucks the gasoline into the cylinder.

intake valve

cylinder

piston

Step 2: Compression Stroke

The piston moves up in the cylinder and compresses, or squeezes, the air and gasoline together.

Step 3: Power Stroke

A small electrical spark causes the gasoline and air to explode. The force of the explosion pushes the piston down again.

The movement of the piston creates energy that makes other parts of the automobile move.

spark plug

Step 4: Exhaust Stroke

The exhaust valve opens and releases gases into the air.

exhaust valve

Chapter 3

The Birth of an Industry

Because the gasoline-powered engine was so successful, many new car companies were started in the United States, and the automobile **industry** was born. An industry is a group of businesses that make the same type of product.

In 1893 Charles E. and J. Frank Duryea built the first gasoline-powered car. In 1895 the American brothers started their own car company.

The Assembly Line

Some people consider Ransom E. Olds to be the founder of the automobile industry. In 1901 Olds **manufactured** (made a product in a factory) over 400 cars. In large factories, Olds used **assembly lines** to make the automobiles.

On an assembly line, workers stood in one place while another worker used a wheeled cart to bring the parts they needed. The workers had special tasks that they would repeat many times, so they were able to do their job quickly. Because of the assembly line, more cars could be manufactured in less time.

Ransom E. Olds

Mass Production

Making cars on an assembly line was cheaper and faster, and by 1903, thousands of cars were being made in Olds' Detroit, Michigan, factory. His method of **mass production**, a process in which items are produced in large quantities, was used by other car companies to produce cars cheaply and in large numbers. Olds' success led many new car companies to join the automobile industry.

The Horseless Carriage

In 1901 Olds introduced the Curved Dash, a car that looked very similar to a carriage. It was called a Curved Dash because the floorboards of the car curved up to form a dashboard.

In 1905 Olds promised $1,000 to the first person who could drive a Curved Dash across the United States from New York to Oregon. The winning racers arrived in Oregon after 45 days.

Detroit, Michigan

In the early 1900s, Detroit, Michigan, became the center of the U.S. automobile industry. Car companies used the Detroit River to gain access to the Great Lakes, and from there it was easy to ship materials to the factories by boat.

Detroit had a large number of workers who were skilled at building machines and carriages, and many of these workers got jobs in automobile factories. By 1910 the population of Detroit had grown to 466,000, and by 1930, 1.5 million people lived in the city.

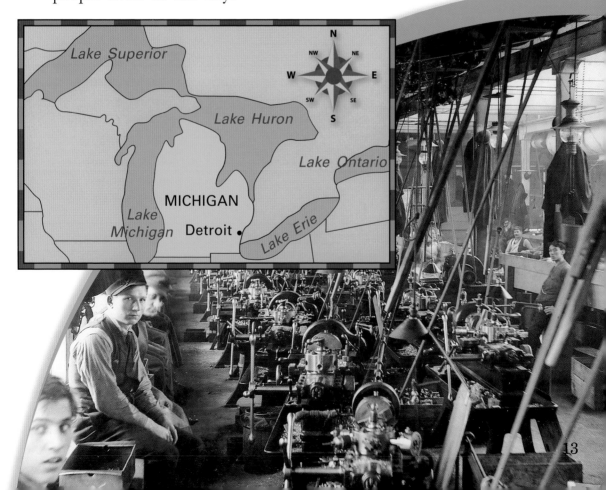

Chapter 4

Famous Ford and His Model T

In 1903 Henry Ford joined the automobile industry and founded Ford Motor Company. Ford wanted to make a car that would be able to handle the tough American country roads, be easy to drive, and be inexpensive to repair.

In 1908 Ford completed his dream car: the Model T. Model Ts were very popular because they were lightweight, affordable, and could carry passengers.

Henry Ford's Model T made owning a car possible for more people because of its low cost and toughness on country roads.

The Moving Assembly Line

Most people believe that Henry Ford perfected mass production by using a moving assembly line in his car factory in 1913. In a moving assembly line, a long, strong chain pulled a Model T car frame through the factory. Workers stood on both sides of the car frame and attached parts that they received from conveyor belts—machines that carried the parts through the factory. The moving assembly line helped Ford Motor Company make three times as many Model Ts in a year than it had before.

Mass production also lowered the costs of making the Model T. The price of a Model T dropped from $950 in 1909 to just $290 in 1922. For more than 20 years, more Model Ts were sold to Americans than any other car, and more than 15 million Model Ts were built.

After the invention of the moving assembly line, it took workers only 93 minutes to build one Model T.

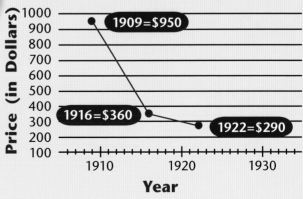

The Price of a Model T

Price (in Dollars)

1909=$950

1916=$360

1922=$290

Year

15

Chapter 5

Electric Power

People were very interested in discovering a way to put cars into motion without using dangerous and smelly gas. While most of the auto industry in the United States was involved in producing cars that were powered by gasoline, a man from Iowa, William Morrison, was working with a different type of energy.

Around 1891 Morrison built the first electric car, which was powered by batteries that were stored under the seats. Many people preferred the electric car to the gas-powered car's smelly fumes and noisy engine, so by the late 1800s, Americans drove more electric cars than gas-powered cars.

an electric car

This woman is showing how to recharge a car battery.

However people soon got tired of having to recharge the batteries every 50 miles. Car buyers also wanted cars that traveled faster, and the electric car's slow speed of 20 miles per hour wasn't fast enough. In contrast, gas-powered cars were more powerful and cheaper to operate, so in the early 1900s, electric car sales began to decrease, and by the 1920s, electric cars were almost completely gone.

Chapter 6

A Changing Industry

The next several years brought many changes to the automobile industry. After companies became experts at mass-producing cars, they started to improve the way cars worked. Inventors, engineers, and car companies quickly made technological advances in engines, car bodies, and the interiors of cars.

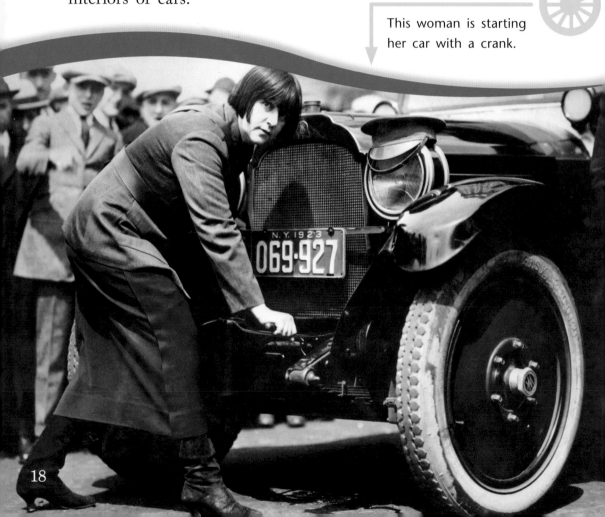

This woman is starting her car with a crank.

A Safe Start

To start an engine, a driver had to put a metal rod, called a crank, into the front of the engine and turn it by hand. This was often dangerous because the crank would sometimes get stuck, and the running engine would spin the crank around and around, hurting the driver.

This changed in 1911 when Charles F. Kettering invented the electric self-starter. With a self-starter, cars could be started mechanically and hand cranks were no longer needed. In 1912 General Motors installed the first self-starters in their Cadillacs.

a Cadillac from the early 1900s

World War I

Though cars were still produced between the years 1914 and 1918, car companies focused on making vehicles to help fight World War I. Factories produced military trucks, tanks, and airplane engines. Ford's Model Ts were used as ambulances during the war. In 1918 the automobile industry made fewer cars for the first time. Materials that were once used to build cars were being used to make military supplies.

The Big Three

In 1919 more than 2 million automobiles were manufactured in the United States, and most of those cars were produced by only three companies: General Motors, founded by William C. Durant; Chrysler Corporation, founded by Walter P. Chrysler; and Ford Motor Company, founded by Henry Ford.

William C. Durant

Walter P. Chrysler

Henry Ford

The 1920s

During the 1920s car companies that couldn't quickly mass produce cars didn't stay in the business for very long. Some leaders of the largest car companies were fired, some companies were sold, and some companies were closed. In 1923 there were 108 car companies, but by 1927, only 44 were still in business.

People wanted cars that not only worked well but also looked good. Some small car companies, such as Rolls Royce and Packard, began to design and build expensive cars that were comfortable to ride in and looked stylish. These cars are now called *classic cars*.

The United Kingdom's Rolls Royce opened a factory in the U.S. to make luxury cars.

Roadside Stops

By 1929 more than 5 million cars were being produced in the United States. Because more people were driving, more businesses were created specifically for travelers. Restaurants were opened along the roadsides, and hotels were built so weary travelers could stop and stay overnight. Gas stations and auto-repair shops were busy repairing cars and keeping them on the road.

Chapter 7

Depression and War

The Great Depression

In the 1930s the United States was hit hard by the Great Depression, a time when the economy was bad, many people were unemployed, and businesses were losing money. The depression greatly affected the automobile industry. Because people didn't have jobs, they couldn't afford to buy cars, and factories had to close. Most car companies lost money during the depression.

UAW

In 1935 the workers in the automobile factories formed a **labor union** called the United Automobile Workers (UAW). A labor union is a group of workers who join together to make sure they receive fair pay and fair treatment from the company that employs them. Today the UAW is one of the largest unions in the United States.

Thousands of people were unemployed during the Great Depression.

World War II

By 1942 the United States was involved in World War II, and car companies were again making products to help fight in the war. The war helped the country recover from the Great Depression by creating jobs, especially for workers in the automobile industry. Workers in car factories made cars, tanks, and airplane engines for the military during World War II.

Cooling Off

In 1940 one car company, Packard Motors, began to include air conditioning in its cars. Soon people could drive in the heat of the summer and still stay cool.

A general purpose vehicle known as the Jeep was used by the military during World War II and eventually became a popular car.

25

Chapter 8

The Post-War Years
Buying for Looks

As soldiers returned from the war, and the economy grew in the United States, many people were ready to buy cars again, and the automobile industry benefited from the huge demand. People wanted to buy cars that not only drove well but also looked good. Cars became larger, longer, and lower to the ground.

Many cars looked like airplanes or rocket ships because of the fins on the back. Cars were more comfortable to ride in and included features such as convertible tops that folded down behind the back seats.

Cadillac Eldorado

Chevrolet Corvette

Chrysler Imperial

A National Highway System

President Dwight D. Eisenhower wanted to establish a national system of highways, so in 1956, the U.S. Congress approved the Federal-Aid Highway Act. Over $25 billion dollars were budgeted to build over 41,000 miles of highway, and the government would pay 90 percent of the cost.

Ford Falcon

Volkswagen Beetle

Chevrolet Corvair

The Birth of the Compact Car

In the late 1950s cars made in Europe were being imported into the United States. Volkswagen, a German car company, began selling Beetles, which were small cars that were sturdy and efficient. At a time when most cars on the road were large and stylish, the Beetle was popular because it was small, affordable, and reliable. Because of the Beetle's popularity, the big U.S. car companies began to make small cars, called compacts, such as the Chevrolet Corvair and the Ford Falcon.

Over 70 percent of families living in the United States owned a car by 1960, and some even owned more than one. There were many types of cars to choose from, though compact cars were very popular. To meet the demands of young car buyers, Ford introduced its first stylish and affordable compact car in 1964: the Ford Mustang. The Ford Mustang was so popular that over 20,000 were bought on the first day they went on sale.

The Ford Mustang is named after a very fast horse.

Chapter 9

The Government Gets More Involved

Cleaning Up

In the 1960s people became more concerned with the negative effects automobiles were having on the environment. The United States was the first country to make laws that limited the amount of pollution allowed from cars.

In 1963 the U.S. government's Clean Air Act required car companies to design engines so that they produced less pollution. The Act has been changed several times to require car companies to reduce pollution even further.

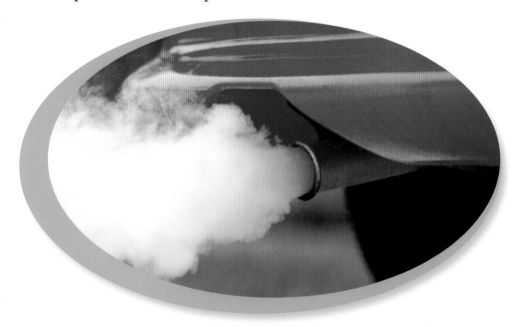

To meet the government's pollution-control guidelines, gasoline was changed as well. A chemical that released harmful lead after gasoline burned in the engine was removed from gasoline. The new formula was called unleaded gasoline. Car companies also made changes to engines to help lower the amount of lead that cars released. Today about 85 percent of cars made use unleaded gasoline.

In the 1970s there was less oil available, so gasoline was much more expensive. As a result, many people began driving smaller cars because smaller cars used less gasoline than larger cars. Imported cars, especially cars from Japan, increased in popularity because they were small and used less gas.

Because of the limited amount of oil and high gas prices, in 1975, the U.S. Congress passed a law that required car companies to make cars that used less gas. In 1974 most cars traveled 14 miles per gallon of gas. But under the new law, by 1985, cars would have to travel almost 28 miles per gallon.

Japanese Cars in the United States

Because people preferred smaller cars to larger ones, Japan became the world's largest automobile manufacturer in 1980. Hundreds of Japanese-made cars were being imported into the United States while the large U.S. car companies were losing money.

As a result, the U.S. government requested that the Japanese government set limits on the number of cars that Japanese car companies could export to the United States each year. These limits ended in 1994.

Staying Safe

Before the 1960s, there weren't many government regulations about the safety of automobiles. However, that changed when the government established the **National Highway Traffic Safety Administration**, or NHTSA.

The main goal of the NHTSA is to reduce deaths and injuries from car crashes. The NHTSA sets safety standards for cars and car equipment, gives money to states for highway safety programs, and provides public information on safety issues. It also does crash tests.

During a crash test, crash-test dummies, which are made to look like people, are placed in a car, and the car crashes into a wall. Engineers use the crash tests to find out how safe different cars are and how the crash affects the crash-test dummies.

Safety Features

Air bags and seatbelts help keep drivers and passengers safe inside a car, but the outside of a car does just as much to keep people safe. Bumpers—the strips on the back and the front of a car—absorb most of the energy when one car hits another car.

The bodies of most cars are made out of materials that will move when they hit something else. The frame that surrounds the car is also made to resist breaking during an accident, leaving a safe area within the car for the driver and passengers.

Chapter 10

Cars Today and in the Future

Trucks and SUVs

Since the 1990s, light trucks and sport utility vehicles (SUVs) have become more popular. The huge demand for these types of automobiles has helped to increase U.S. car companies' profits, and U.S. car companies have produced more trucks and SUVs than any other car.

The bar graph and circle graph below show the number of automobiles sold in 2003 by one car company.

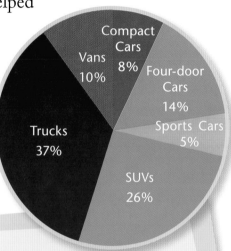

Compact Cars 8%
Vans 10%
Four-door Cars 14%
Sports Cars 5%
SUVs 26%
Trucks 37%

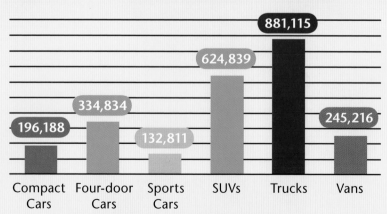

Sales of Automobiles – 2003

Number of Automobiles

Kinds of Automobiles	Number of Automobiles
Compact Cars	196,188
Four-door Cars	334,834
Sports Cars	132,811
SUVs	624,839
Trucks	881,115
Vans	245,216

Cars of the Future

Future inventions will make cars more comfortable, faster, and safer. Engines will use less gas and produce less pollution. Computers will become even more important in cars. In fact, many cars today already have small computers that provide maps and directions. However, the most important future development in cars will probably involve how a car gets its energy.

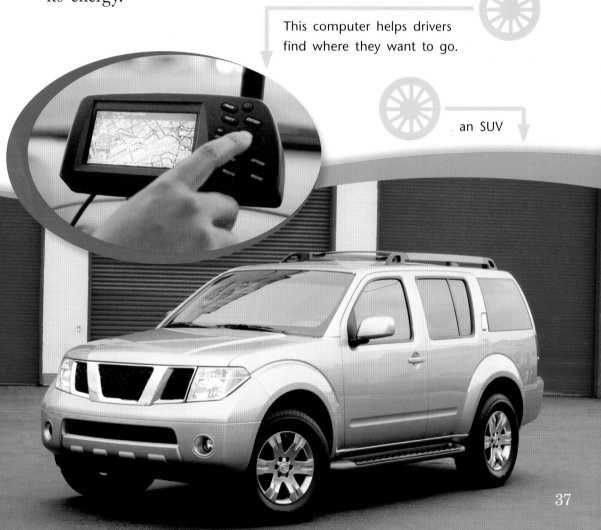

This computer helps drivers find where they want to go.

an SUV

Today there are several different hybrid cars, which are powered by a combination of gasoline and batteries. They have smaller engines that use less gas and produce much less pollution than other cars. Though hybrid cars use less fuel than gas-powered cars, they are very expensive to make and repair. In 1997 the Japanese car company Toyota began making the Toyota Prius, which was the first mass-produced hybrid car.

Toyota Prius

From the steam car to the hybrid car, automobiles have changed a lot since their beginning. Car companies have worked to make cars more comfortable, better-looking, and easier to drive. Laws have been passed to set limits on pollution and standards for safety. Technology has made cars safer, more fuel-efficient, and friendlier to the environment.

What will happen next?

Glossary

assembly line a method in which workers stand in one place and repeat a special task to put something together

industry a group of businesses that make the same type of product

labor union a group of workers who join together to make sure they receive fair pay and fair treatment from the company that employs them

manufacture to make a product by hand or by machine, usually in a factory

mass production producing many items in large quantities

National Highway Traffic Safety Administration (NHTSA) the government organization that is responsible for setting automobile safety standards

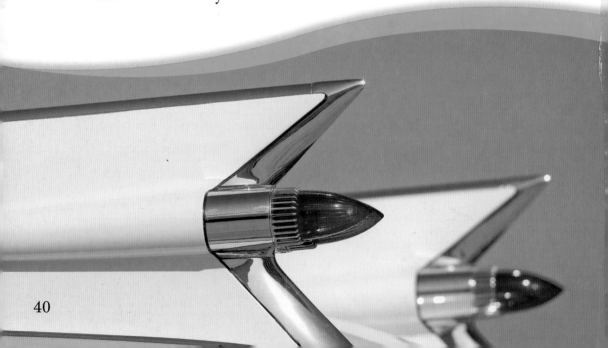